Simply Weddings

22 of the Most Requested Pieces for Wedding Ceremonies

Arranged by Dan Fox

Simply Weddings is a collection of famous masterpieces by some of the most influential composers in history. These selections have been featured in wedding ceremonies time and again due to their great popularity. They have been carefully arranged by Dan Fox for Easy Piano, making them accessible to pianists of all ages. Phrase markings, articulations, fingering, dynamics, and pedaling have been included to aid with interpretation, and a large print size makes the notation easy to read.

Music plays a vital part in wedding ceremonies, creating the right atmosphere as guests arrive and highlighting important moments during the service. Johann Sebastian Bach's *Arioso* or his *Jesu, Joy of Man's Desiring* provide gentle background music for the entrance of the wedding party. Johann Pachelbel's *Canon* or Richard Wagner's famous *Bridal Chorus* signal the grand entrance of the bride. Serene works such as Franz Schubert's *Ave Maria* or Frédéric Chopin's *Nocturne* are perfect accompaniments to the lighting of the unity candle or other special moments during the ceremony. Henry Purcell's *Recessional* or Felix Mendelssohn's *Wedding March* provide a jubilant fanfare as the couple is presented to their friends and family and departs. Additionally, wedding music is a joy to play on the piano. The melodies are unforgettable and can rekindle fond memories. For these reasons and more, the masterpieces on the following pages are exciting to explore.

After all, this is *Simply Weddings!*

Cover illustration by Sarah Vaughan

Contents

Gymnopédie

Erik Satie (1866–1925)
Arranged by Dan Fox

Slow and mournful

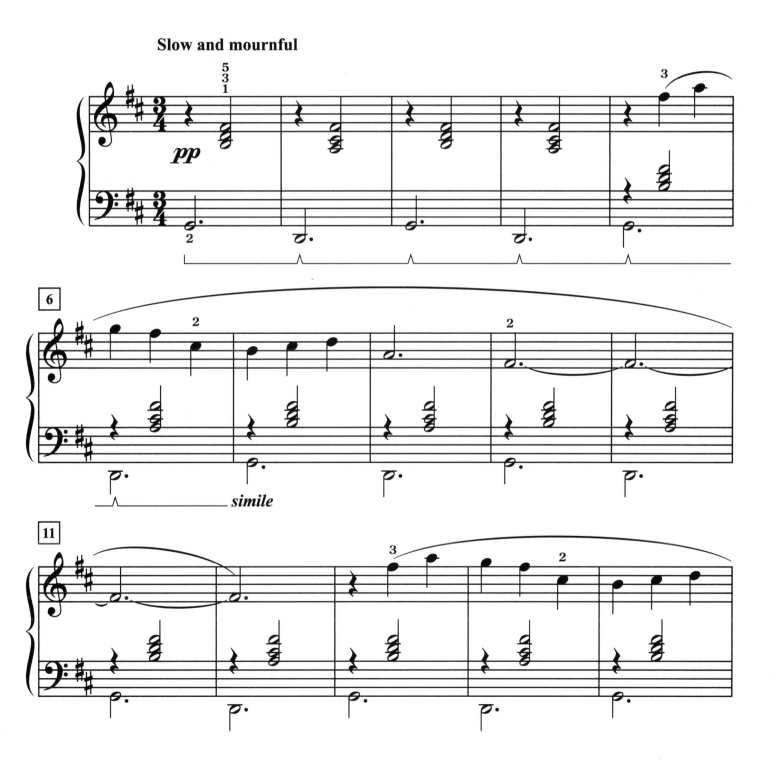

4

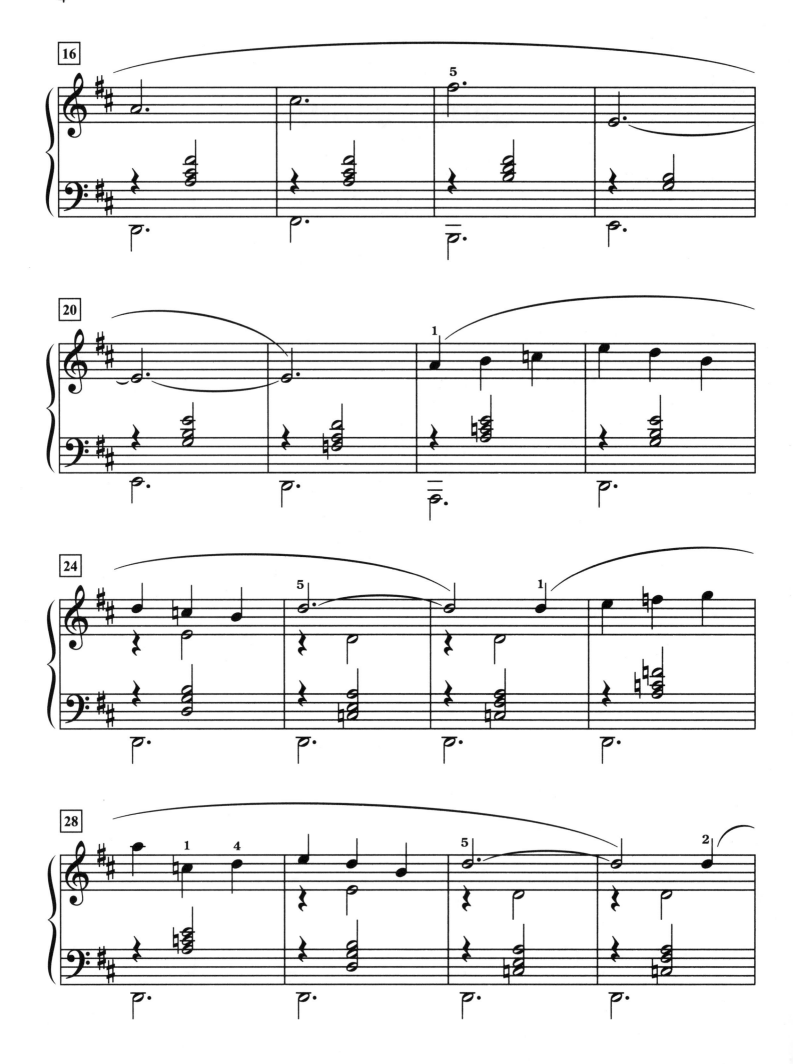

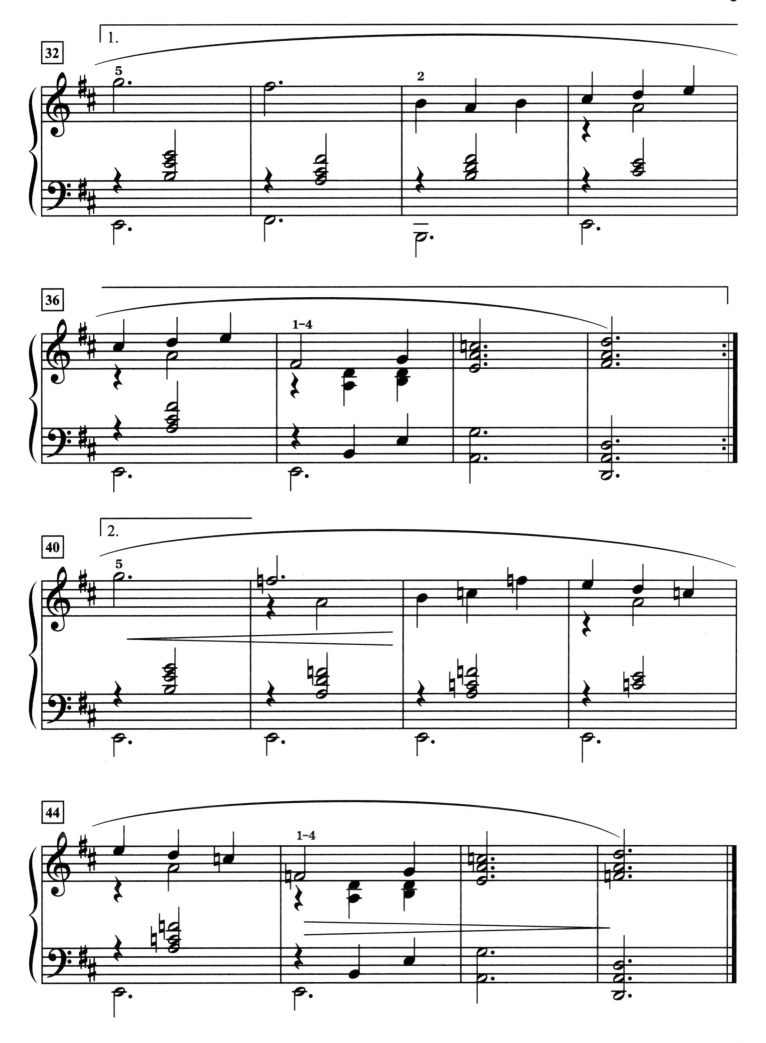

Allegro maestoso

(from *Water Music*)

George Frideric Handel (1685–1759)
Arranged by Dan Fox

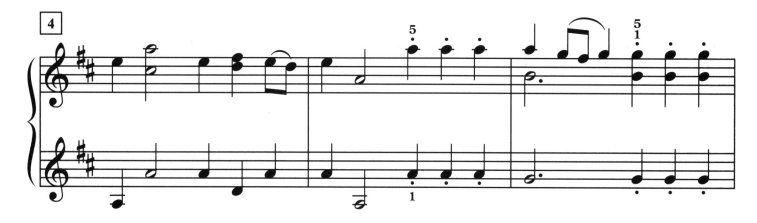

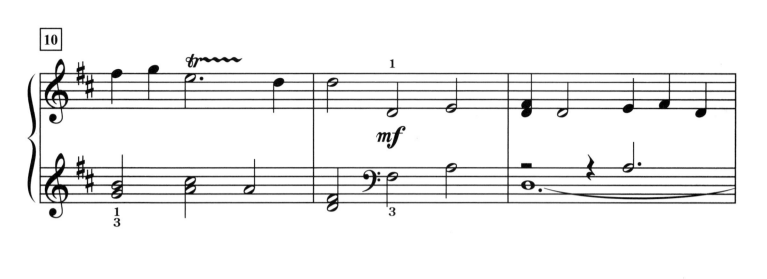

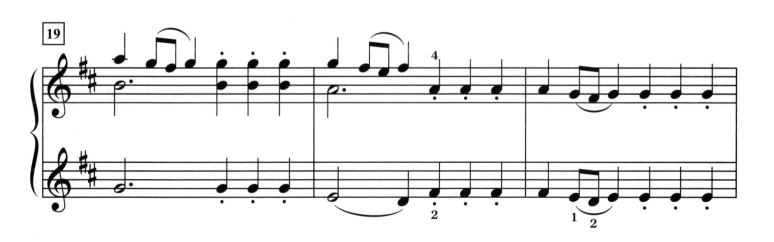

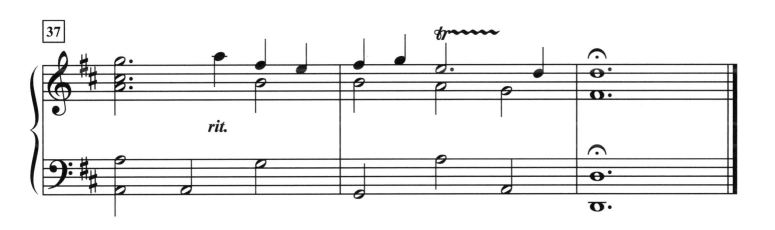

Arioso

Johann Sebastian Bach (1685–1750)
Arranged by Dan Fox

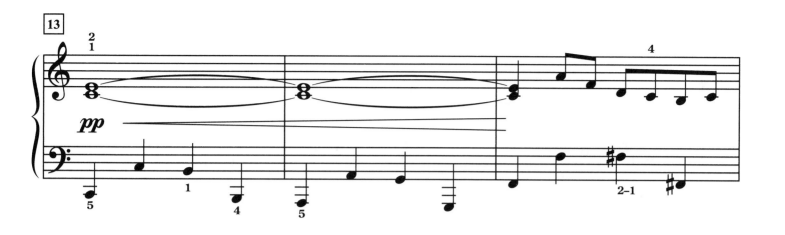

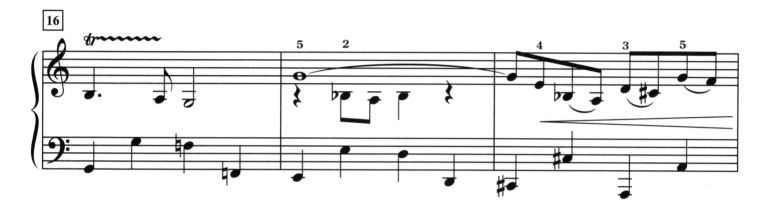

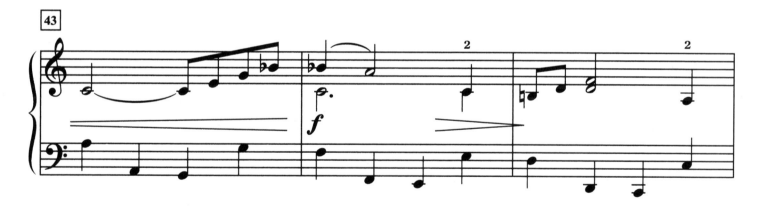

Ave Maria

Charles Gounod (1818–1893)
Based on *Prelude in C Major*
by J. S. Bach (1685–1750)
Arranged by Dan Fox

Moderato

simile

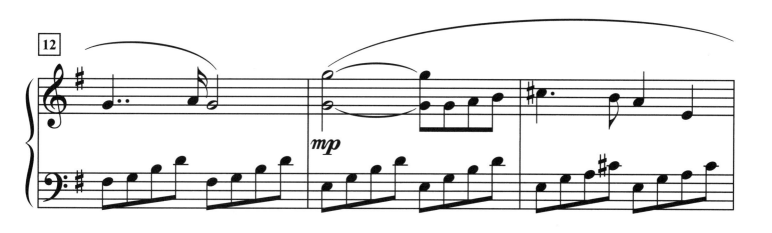

Ave Maria

Franz Schubert (1797–1828)
Arranged by Dan Fox

Slowly, with great reverence

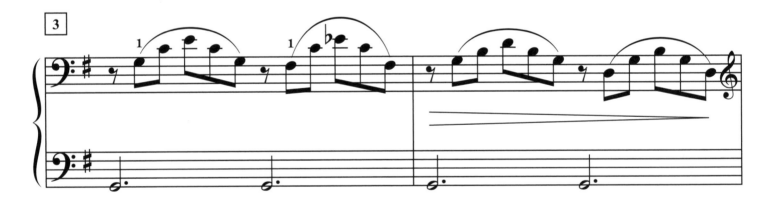

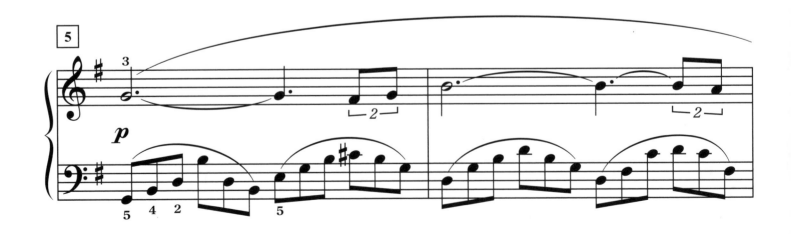

Barcarolle

(from *The Tales of Hoffman*)

Jacques Offenbach (1819–1880)
Arranged by Dan Fox

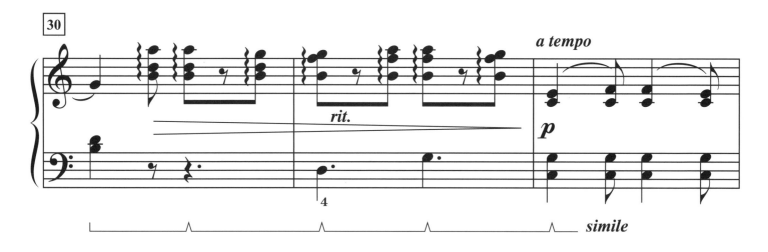

Be Thou with Me

(Bist Du bei Mir)

Johann Sebastian Bach (1685–1750)
Arranged by Dan Fox

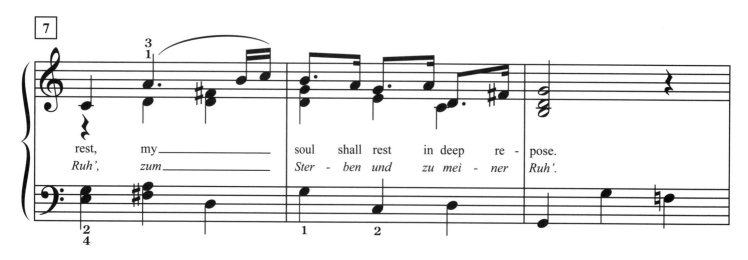

Bridal Chorus

(from *Lohengrin*)

Richard Wagner (1813–1883)
Arranged by Dan Fox

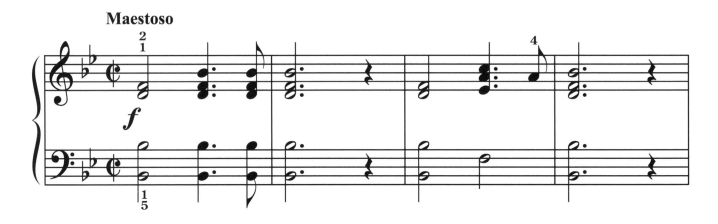

Canon

Johann Pachelbel (1653–1706)
Arranged by Dan Fox

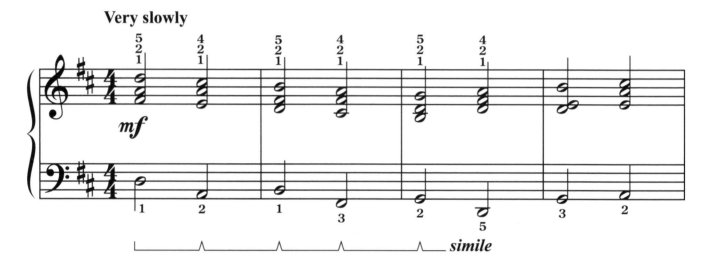

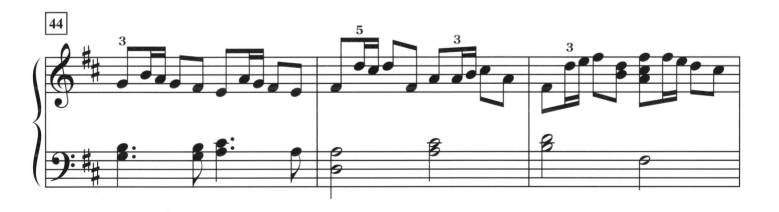

* The RH chord may be played an octave higher.

Jesu, Joy of Man's Desiring

Johann Sebastian Bach (1685–1750)
Arranged by Dan Fox

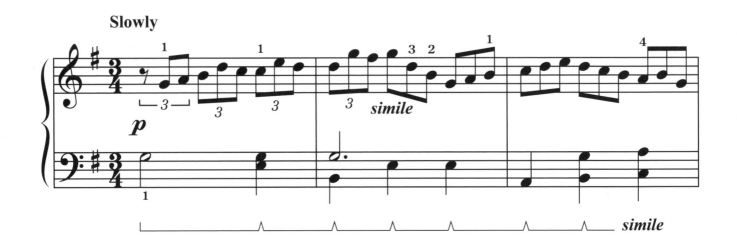

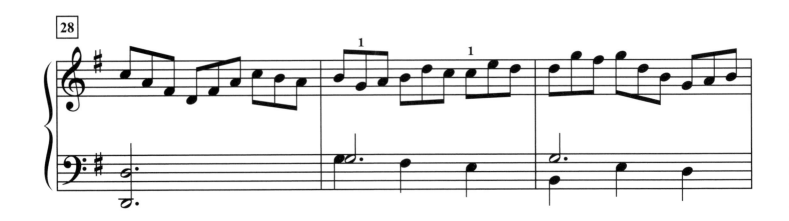

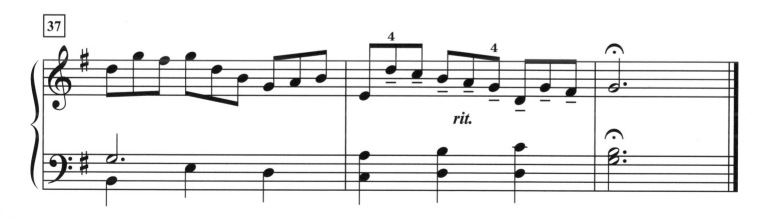

Larghetto

George Frideric Handel (1685–1759)
Arranged by Dan Fox

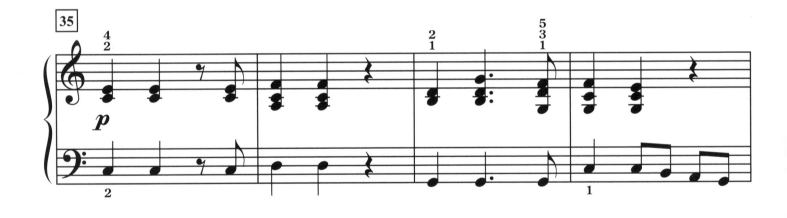

Nocturne

(from *String Quartet in D*)

Alexander Borodin (1833–1887)
Arranged by Dan Fox

Moderately slow

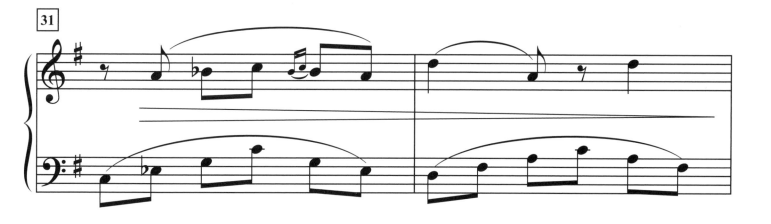

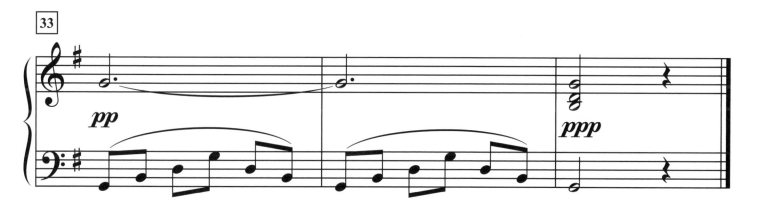

Nocturne

Frédéric Chopin (1810–1849)
Arranged by Dan Fox

Moderately slow

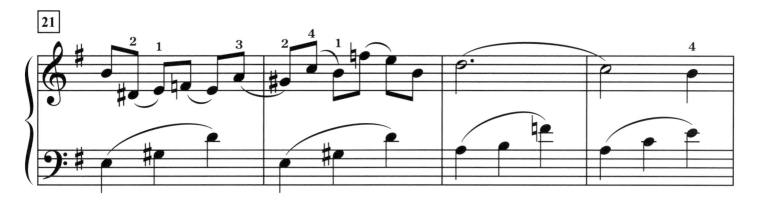

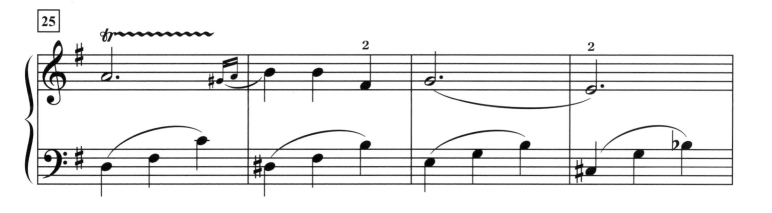

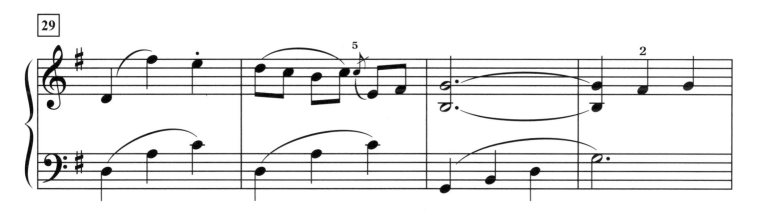

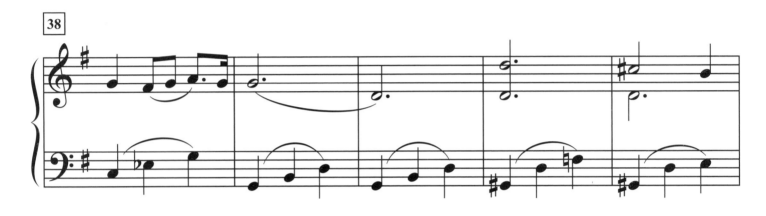

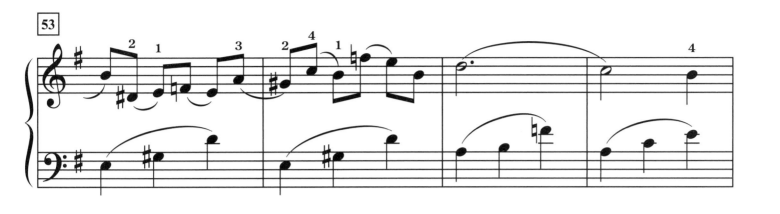

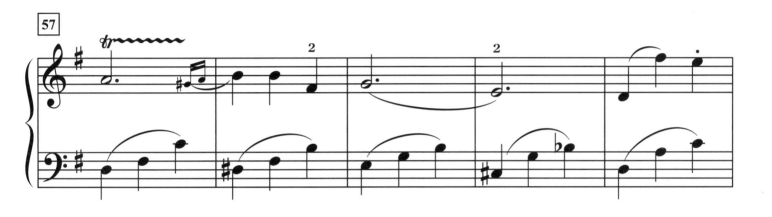

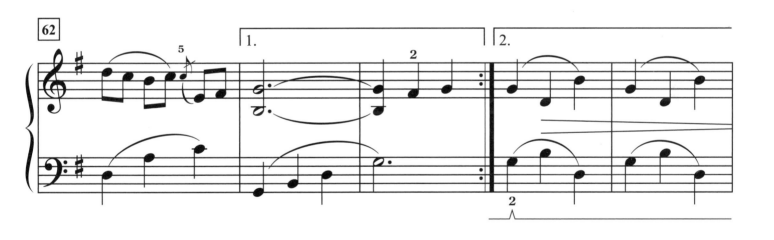

O mio babbino caro

(from *Gianni Schicchi*)

Giacomo Puccini (1858–1924)
Arranged by Dan Fox

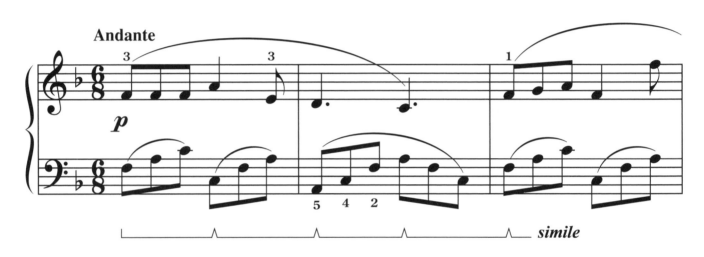

Ode to Joy

(from *Symphony No. 9*)

Ludwig van Beethoven (1770–1827)
Arranged by Dan Fox

Allegro con spirito

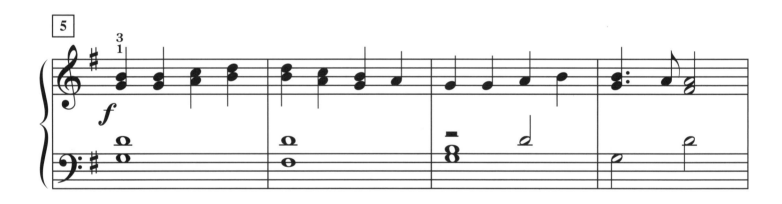

Panis Angelicus

César Franck (1822–1890)
Arranged by Dan Fox

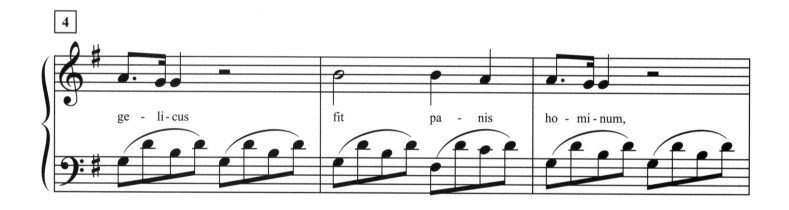

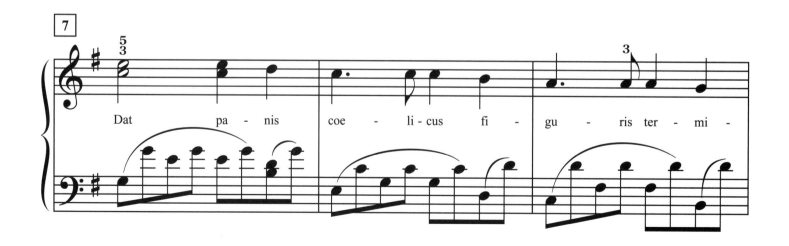

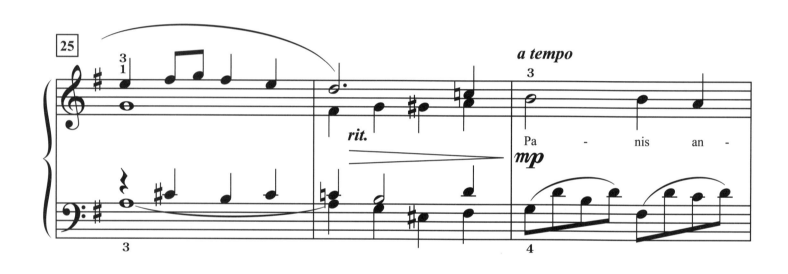

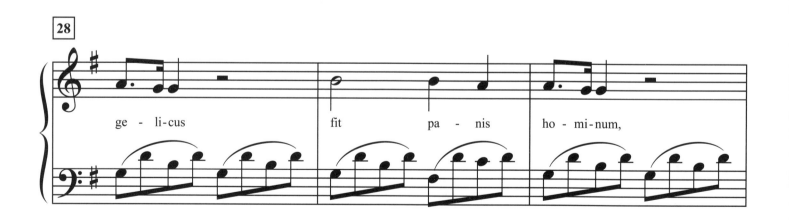

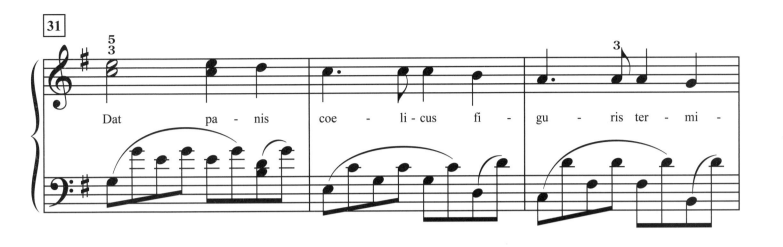

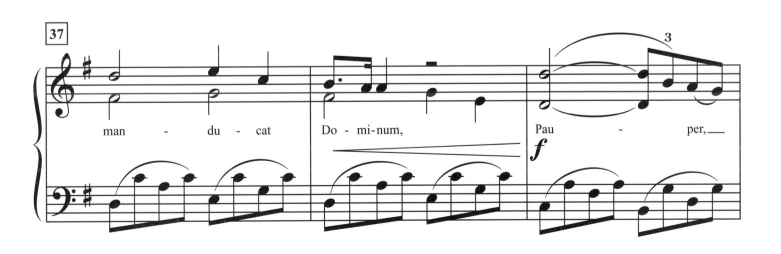

Plaisir d'amour

Giovanni Battista Martini (1706–1784)
Arranged by Dan Fox

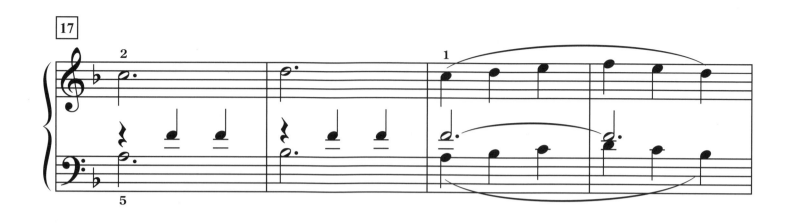

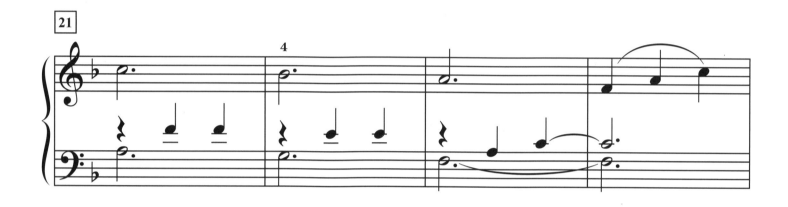

Recessional

Henry Purcell (1659–1695)
Arranged by Dan Fox

Maestoso moderato

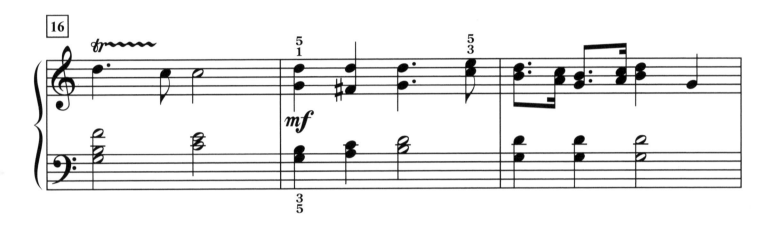

Rhapsody on a Theme of Paganini
(18th Variation)

Sergei Rachmaninoff (1873–1943)
Arranged by Dan Fox

Moderately slow

Sheep May Safely Graze

Johann Sebastian Bach (1685–1750)
Arranged by Dan Fox

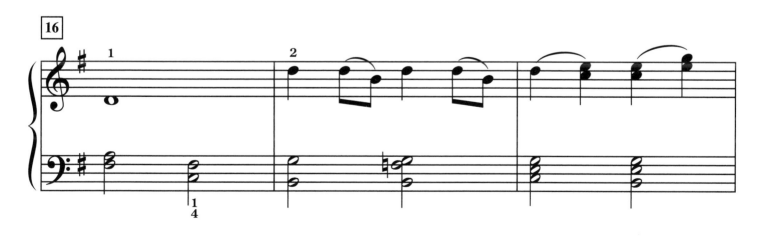

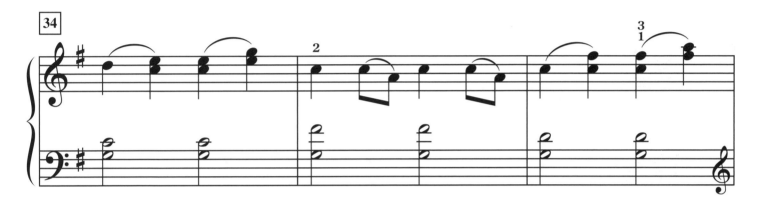

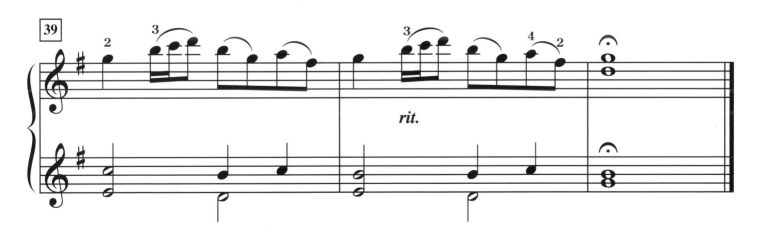

Trumpet Voluntary
(The Prince of Denmark's March)

Jeremiah Clarke (1673–1707)
Arranged by Dan Fox

Wedding March

Felix Mendelssohn (1809–1847)
Arranged by Dan Fox

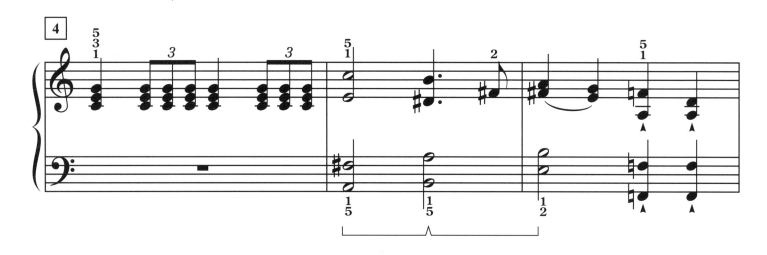

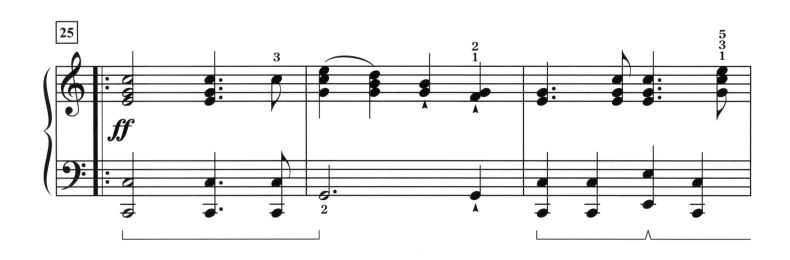